suffering and realized the true, natural state of the Self, Brahman, which is of the nature of pure Being-Consciousness-Bliss.

This booklet is intended as a pithy reminder of some salient points regarding these requisites in the context of Self-inquiry.

The four requisites are: discrimination, detachment, the six essentials, and the desire for Liberation. The six essentials are peacefulness, self-control, renunciation or nondependence, endurance or fortitude, faith or conviction, and profound, concentrated, formless meditation. The original significance of them and the actual experience of them for those on the path of Knowledge are far-reaching.

Each of the four requisites is helpful to the inquiry to know the Self. Each of the four requisites supports the others. The order in which they are given is not to be construed as being strictly developmental or ascending. For example, though one requires discrimination to become detached (otherwise, one will not perceive who is to be detached and from what to be detached), it may be the desire for Liberation coupled with conviction in the teachings that give rise to that discrimination, which is further strengthened by meditation and expressed through some kind of renunciation on a basis of peacefulness or equanimity. Each may be considered separately, or they may be considered as one whole.

These requisites for Realization are to be understood, meditated upon, and practiced within the context of Nonduality for the purpose of Self-Realization. They can also be practiced, at least to a certain extent, by those who have as yet to ascertain that Nonduality is Truth, that Realization consists of Self-Knowledge, and that the means, which is Self-inquiry, must be in accord with or of the same nature as the end, that is, Self-Realization. Here, an understanding of this on the part of the aspirant is assumed and the four requisites for Realization are taught with special relevance to Self-inquiry, the introspective determination of the true nature of one's own Self, which is the Absolute Self.

The Four Requisites for Realization and Self-inquiry

(Sadhana Chatushtaya and Atma Vichara)

Since very ancient times, seekers yearning for Self-Realization, or Enlightenment, have sought instruction to assist them. Instruction from genuine sages established in the Knowledge of the Self has generally been in two ways: instruction about the nature of the Self, the Absolute, and instruction regarding the way to abide in, or realize, this Supreme Knowledge. The latter forms the instruction regarding a path or spiritual practice.

In the Teaching of Nonduality, which clearly reveals the identity of the Self and the Absolute (Brahman, God), Liberation or Self-Realization is recognized to be of the nature of Self-Knowledge. A path of Knowledge results in Self-Knowledge, and the primary method of the path is that of Self-inquiry. The inquiry is the introspection, or meditation, that ascertains in the most experiential manner what it is of which one's true identity consists. It is the self-revelation of the nature of Being, or Consciousness itself, unobscured by any definition or mis-identification. Questing inwardly as to "Who am I?" one realizes one's true state of Nondual Existence, which is ever free, ever at peace, immutable, without modifications, illimitable, timeless, indivisible, forever unconditioned, formless, undifferentiated—the One Reality.

In practice, the actual inquiry, itself, involves the relinquishment of the false superimposition of forms and attributes upon the Self. This involves the recognition of the false definition and the discernment of how it is not actually one's identity. It is the shifting of identity from where it has been misplaced, such as being associated with the body or with thought, and restoring it to its natural position, which is the Self alone. It is the ceasing of the confusion regarding what is real and what is unreal, so that the erroneous attribution of reality to the unreality, such as conceiving the world, objects, events, sensations, and thoughts to be real or to be the means of determining what is real, is relinquished.

The Four Requisites for Realization and Self-inquiry

(Sadhana Chatushtaya and Atma Vichara)

Since very ancient times, seekers yearning for Self-Realization, or Enlightenment, have sought instruction to assist them. Instruction from genuine sages established in the Knowledge of the Self has generally been in two ways: instruction about the nature of the Self, the Absolute, and instruction regarding the way to abide in, or realize, this Supreme Knowledge. The latter forms the instruction regarding a path or spiritual practice.

In the Teaching of Nonduality, which clearly reveals the identity of the Self and the Absolute (Brahman, God), Liberation or Self-Realization is recognized to be of the nature of Self-Knowledge. A path of Knowledge results in Self-Knowledge, and the primary method of the path is that of Self-inquiry. The inquiry is the introspection, or meditation, that ascertains in the most experiential manner what it is of which one's true identity consists. It is the self-revelation of the nature of Being, or Consciousness itself, unobscured by any definition or mis-identification. Questing inwardly as to "Who am I?" one realizes one's true state of Nondual Existence, which is ever free, ever at peace, immutable, without modifications, illimitable, timeless, indivisible, forever unconditioned, formless, undifferentiated—the One Reality.

In practice, the actual inquiry, itself, involves the relinquishment of the false superimposition of forms and attributes upon the Self. This involves the recognition of the false definition and the discernment of how it is not actually one's identity. It is the shifting of identity from where it has been misplaced, such as being associated with the body or with thought, and restoring it to its natural position, which is the Self alone. It is the ceasing of the confusion regarding what is real and what is unreal, so that the erroneous attribution of reality to the unreality, such as conceiving the world, objects, events, sensations, and thoughts to be real or to be the means of determining what is real, is relinquished.

Discrimination

Discrimination refers to the ability to discern what is true and what is not true. It may commence with deep thinking or contemplation, yet as it becomes clear and firm, it is a matter of actual inner experience. It may start with what is very basic, yet continues to be instrumental in the Knowledge until Realization itself. Unless a person discerns the source of happiness, is there much of a possibility of finding that happiness, let alone retaining it without subsequent loss? Unless a person discerns the purpose of life, will it be fulfilled? It is only for a person exercising keen discrimination regarding what constitutes Realization that a corresponding clear way of realizing will become evident. Otherwise, the seeker will practice in a random fashion that more often than not will correlate to unexamined ignorant tendencies rather than serve to destroy such delusive notions and patterns of conceptualizing. How will it be possible for one to know oneself without releasing the misidentifications that currently bind or obscure him? And how will it be possible to thoroughly release such misidentifications unless they are discerned as being such rather than being assumed to be one's actual nature, which is the Absolute Self?

Discrimination enables one to know Reality as it is. If ignorance consists of taking the Real to be unreal and the unreal to be real, one must discern which is real and which is unreal in order to be free of ignorance. Freedom from ignorance is true Knowledge, the nonconceptual wisdom that sees Reality as it is. This discrimination cannot be a sensory activity. As long as one assumes that the senses determine what is, so long one imagines a supposed external world to be existent and objects to be real. The senses display only minute sensations—minute and momentary no matter how varied, complex, or large they may appear to be—and not the ever-present Existence as it is. The senses are incapable of determining the real nature of the Existence that is the Self. One cannot expect to see the formless Self, to hear the silent Self, to touch the intangible Self, etc. Moreover, what is real must always be so in order to be real. If it is not so, a thing is entirely unreal or a misperception of what is real. The transient senses are incapable of perceiving the eternal Reality. The Self which one seeks to realize is the eternal Reality. Therefore, the inquiry utilizing discrimination to know the Self is not a sensory activity, does not depend on the senses, eliminates the belief in the validity or reality of the sensory "perceptions," and reveals the sense-transcendent Self. It is in this light that Sankara's statement that discrimination is the understanding that Brahman (the vast Absolute) is reality and the material world is false (mithya) becomes experientially understood.

Though the discrimination may commence with thinking, in actual practice, it does not remain as just thought. The Self is not a thought; nor is it all the thoughts gathered together. To confound thought with the Self is ignorance. No thought can be ever-existent, limitless, utterly formless, and eternal. No thought is actually Consciousness, which is the Self. Discrimination discerns the Self and thus reveals its freedom from thought. With discrimination, one comprehends that Consciousness is the unaffected Witness of all thought and cannot be a thought, and, by this discrimination, one is no longer bound by thought. Profound discrimination reveals the existence of Consciousness alone and the fact that there is really no such existent thing as thought.

This process of discernment, from the most basic to the finest discrimination, actually uses something inherent in and natural to everyone. Everyone knows if he is happy or not. Everyone knows that he exists. How is it that everyone has this intrinsic discernment? It is because Knowledge is of the very nature of the Self. The aspirant for Liberation can very well use this intrinsic ability, an ability that is interior and unfailing, for the purpose of inquiring to know the Self.

The path to Self-Knowledge is, itself, composed of Knowledge. The inquiry to become undefined is in perfect accord with it, for to remain undefined is to be in one's natural state. This requisite of discrimination, likewise, is of the nature of Knowledge. Advancement in this path is a matter of Knowledge, and the spiritual experiences, from beginning to Realization, are of the nature of Knowledge.

To commence discrimination, one may start meditation with what are seemingly simple questions, such as, "What is the source of happiness? What is eternal? What is real? Who am I?" Though simple and basic, these questions remain extremely useful continually in the practice. The significance of these questions deepens in direct proportion to the depth of discrimination. The discrimination may very well manifest as a sorting process, with more emphasis usually on the negation of what is not eternal, not Reality, or not the Self, resulting in the eternal Reality of the Self being left unobscured and self-evident by virtue of the discrimination.

The discrimination should also be applied to one's view of Realization in order to free such of dualistic conceptions. Furthermore, the discrimination must be applied to one's own practices in order to sort out what is actually fruitful and what not in the effort to realize the Self. Considering how short life is and how important it is to apply oneself fully, it is imperative to, again and again, clarify ones comprehension of the path so that effort is wisely applied and fruitful.

The distinguishing of what is helpful and what is a hindrance to spiritual development is a result of discrimination. The spiritual discernment of what action is beneficial and what is deleterious, the law of karma, as well as transcendence of karma, which can occur only in Knowledge and not physically or in bodily terms, are a result of discrimination. The distinguishing of the causes of emotional moods and how to liberate oneself from them is a result of discrimination. The discernment of mental tendencies and concepts and disidentifying from them is a matter of discrimination. The destruction of the manifest egoistic tendencies or misidentifications and the realization of the absence of the ego altogether is of the nature of discrimination. All the aspects of liberating oneself from misidentifications, or superimpositions of the non-Self upon the Self, and ascertaining what is true about the Self depend upon the ability called, "spiritual discrimination."

Discrimination may manifest as a practice of comparison and contrast in meditation and as the elimination of the superimposition of various things and ideas upon the Self, which alone is the source of happiness, one's identity, and Reality. Discrimination causes these—happiness, identity, and reality—to be known where they truly abide: as One and as the Self alone. This comparing and contrasting takes the form of discerning the immutable from the changeful, the eternal from the transitory, the continuous from the sporadic, the nonobjective from the objective, the nondependent from the dependent, the indivisible from the multiple or divisible, and by similar distinctions between the real Self and the unreal misidentifications or things with which one misidentifies. At its zenith, discrimination reveals that which has been negated as utterly nonexistent and that the Reality alone is.

Discrimination should not be wrongly associated with mere intellectual learning, cogitation, and opining. On the contrary, discrimination reveals that which is beyond the intellect, what is not a product of thought, and destroys the personal opinions of the pseudo-entity, the ego, to reveal what actually exists. In practice, discrimination may be subtle or vivid revelation, but it always signifies a shift in what one feels one's identity is. If one supposedly knows better but cannot live up to it, sees attachment but cannot abandon it, recognizes a binding emotion but continues to dwell in it, understands a concept to be such but continues to misidentify with it, such is a lack of discrimination or Knowledge. Indeed, such means that one has only added the new term to the old delusion, illusion, bondage, and suffering. That is not discrimination. No such thing occurs in real discrimination, just as one does not run for water in a mirage when one knows it to be a mirage, does not touch something burning hot when one knows it be hot, and is not fooled or frightened by a supposed snake when one knows it to be only a rope.

Spiritual discrimination may come quickly or slowly, in a flash or after repeated contemplation and meditation, entirely on one's own or after detailed instruction. None of that is of any consequence. What is essential is that one develops the ability to keenly discern. Without such discrimination, the light of Wisdom, or Knowledge, will not dawn, even though the Reality is ever present and within oneself.

Spiritual discrimination reveals the Truth, which transcends all forms and actions, all words and thought. The aspirant should exercise discrimination to arrive at the actual experience and true meaning of the teachings of sages, using one's best reasoning powers for an innermost purpose. The seeing of the Self beyond all notions is a result of discrimination.

It is only that which one truly knows that is actually experienced. It is only that which is actually experienced that one truly knows. Spiritual discrimination commences when one abandons any illusory division between understanding and experience, and they are one and simultaneous. The path is the fusion of understanding and experience. One's own existence is simultaneously known and experienced, and it is precisely at such inner depth that spiritual discrimination should be practiced.

Spiritual discrimination gives rise to the other requisites for Realization. It is the cornerstone of spiritual advancement. It is a like a bright lamp taken with one. It illumines the way and in the hunt for shadows, everywhere it is brought, no darkness is seen to exist.

Discrimination is of the very essence of the path of Knowledge, and it is such a way in Knowledge that results in Self-Knowledge.

Detachment

Lack of discernment regarding the real source of happiness and peace, the actual way to be free and contented, the real source of love and satisfaction, and such produces attachment. Attachment produces suffering; indeed, attachment is suffering. Discrimination leads to detachment. Detachment yields freedom and joy; indeed, detachment is freedom and joy.

If discrimination does not lead to detachment, it is not sufficiently deep, and its purpose, which is the experience of lasting happiness remains unfulfilled. Discrimination with detachment leads to Liberation, which is full of bliss and peace. Discrimination yields the ability to become detached, and detachment enables the seeker to become further discriminating.

Detachment comes by clarity regarding the nature of happiness and the nature of that which endures. Attachment occurs due to ignorance regarding the source of happiness and because one believes that that to which one is attached, be it an object, a person, an event, a situation, or any other thing, will endure and never change or perish. Meditation upon the transient nature of all things, relations, events, and situations helps to develop detachment. Further, meditation that ascertains the truth about happiness, be it called peace, satisfaction, love, or by any other term, results in detachment. The seeker of Self-Realization should meditate upon being detached and then meditate with detachment upon the essential inquiry into the Self.

If one is attached, one suffers. It is not possible to be free and truly content as long as one is attached. Attachment creates suffering, obscures wisdom, and gives the false sense of bondage. One should not be confused about attachment and feel that it is integral to love. Love is of the unity of the truth of the nature of all beings, but attachment actually produces an illusion of separation and merely obstructs that very love. Similar is it with the sense of security that one in delusion may regard as dependent on attachment. Attachment makes for the absence of peace, the sense of insecurity. Even if, in delusion, one supposes these provide security or love, the anxiety over these, which is evident to anyone who is discerning, is suffering and a very insecure state. If there is freedom from attachment, peace is present within.

Attachment is a mode of mind and not a particular action or the possession of something. Though renunciation has been used by many spiritual beings to enhance, help, or express their becoming detached, the detachment, itself, is an inner state and not a particular action. With detachment, one can abide free and at peace in the midst of pleasant or unpleasant circumstances, with friends or with those who carry animosity, among others or all alone, with wealth or with poverty, and when active and when inactive.

The greater the detachment, the greater the sense of peace and freedom, even while one still imagines the world to be real or conceives of himself as if in a world. Moreover, the detachment enables the aspirant to meditate on the Truth regarding Existence itself, the Self, and thus transcend the world entirely, including the very notion that it exists or is a reality apart from the Self. No one who is still attached to the things of the world will wish to proceed to meditate on world-transcending Truth for fear of losing what he considers to be the source of happiness and peace and what he conceives to be real. One who is detached, though, is not bound or impeded in such a manner and, free from clinging to particular things, is capable of liberating himself from the entirety of the illusion, discovering by immediate experience that happiness, peace, and reality are of the very nature of the Self.

Detachment is declared to be "from the fruits of action here and hereafter; it is detachment from all worldly things and all heavenly things." The significance is that one who is in pursuit of Self-Knowledge, the Realization of the Absolute, should not have attachment to any material thing, worldly circumstance, or personal relationship of any kind. It also means that one should not be attached to the obtaining of religious reward, whether conceived as being reaped in an after-death state or within the context of that aspect of illusion manifesting as the present life and its experiences. Sri Ramana Maharshi has stated that "here" is to be understood to be everything of the world perceived through the senses and that "hereafter" is to be understood as pertaining to all that is in the mind. The attachments are based on misidentifications and are a hindrance to the destruction of the illusory ego, which is Liberation, or Self-Realization. Therefore, one who yearns for Self-Realization and, thus, seeks to know himself as he truly is will abandon attachment.

Sankara has stated that detachment is "from all transient objects from the body to Brahman" and "from all things seen, heard, and such." The latter phrase means that one has to abide free from attachment to anything perceived by the senses and one must also be detached from the sensing itself, be it seeing, hearing, tasting, smelling, or touching. One should know That within oneself that does not depend on these senses or their objects, and one should discern the wondrous source of happiness within that remains whether or not the senses are appearing. For real freedom and peace, one must be without attachment to, without confusion regarding, the objects that are perceived, which though perceived are yet unreal like the water in a mirage. For real freedom and peace, one must be detached from, nondependent upon, the senses (the sensing), so that whether or not one's senses are functioning, such as able to hear or deaf or able to see or blind, one's abidance in the real source of happiness and peace is undisturbed. For Realization of the Self, one should recognize that the Self, of the nature of Being-Consciousness-Bliss, can never be an object of sensory perception. The Self cannot be seen, heard, tasted, smelled, or felt as a tactile sensation. It has no color or size, no sound, no feeling, no fragrance, and such. The Self is Existence without any such forms and is free from all such transient sensations, be they pleasurable or painful. The path of Knowledge, itself, which is the inquiry into the Self, is not a sensory process. The meditation is not performed by the senses or with the senses as instruments, and the experience that results from inquiry is of Self-Knowledge and not of a sensory character. Using discrimination, if the aspirant has experiences of a sensory character as a result of meditation, such as seeing, hearing, or feeling differently, he will discern that these are transient illusions and will remain detached from them, while continuing the actual inquiry into the Self to know it as it is. The Knowledge of the Self, which is the Knowledge of Reality, actual Existence, is not of a sensory character. Therefore, the seeker of Self-Knowledge who is endowed with detachment understands that the senses are not the means of knowing Reality. The senses are never the measure of Reality. One who comprehends this Knowledge is no longer confused about Reality and remains unattached to the entire world.

The first phrase quoted from Sankara's instruction regarding detachment states that one is to be detached from transient things from the body to Brahman. Just as other objects are dependent upon the senses to even appear, so is it with the body. Just as other objects have a creation and a destruction, so does the body have a birth and a death. Just as there is no happiness inherent in any object, but all joy is of the Self alone, so happiness does not depend upon the body. Just as real

Existence is not perceived as long as one believes in the reality of objects, so one does not know the real Self, which is Existence itself, as long as one misidentifies with the body. Just as sense perception is objective, so the body itself is objective, while the Self is the non objective Consciousness. In this manner, the aspirant should meditate on the Self as being free of the body and its related limitations. One who can discriminate like this becomes detached from the body. The detachment is not physical or subtle and is not any kind of action or change in the condition or state of the body. The detachment is always a state of Knowledge. It is clarity regarding one's identity. Detachment from the body means that one remains free and unperturbed regardless of whatever state the body is in. It is not being senseless as one under anesthesia; it is transcendence, so that, with or without the senses, with or without the body, one abides as Being, and Being remains as it is, unmoved and immutable. In Absolute Being, there are no such things as the senses or bodies. Transcendence means clear Knowledge regarding the truth of one's identity.

"From the body to" means inclusive of everything from the physical to the subtle to the mental to the notion of "I." All that is perceived and conceived is transient. What is the use of being attached to that which can never last anyway? What is transient is not the abiding Reality. What is the use of being attached to the unreal? What is transient is not the Self but is merely witnessed by the Self, of the nature of nonobjective Consciousness. What is the use of imagining a connection with that which can never actually be oneself? What is transient cannot provide lasting happiness and peace. What is the use of continuing to imagine that it can so provide? Even the concept of the Absolute, the concept of "Brahman," is not eternal. Brahman alone knows Brahman in a nonconceptual manner. That is to say, the Self realizes itself in a Knowledge that is not dependent on, or produced by, thought. The idea, "the Self," is not the Self. No idea is the eternal. The eternal Self is beyond any idea. It is more subjective than, or interior to, any idea. There is no need to be attached to one's idea of the Self or the Absolute, for when all ideas are relinquished, the ever present, real Being-Consciousness still remains, self-luminous, self-knowing, replete with its innate Bliss. Complete detachment is Knowledge.

In the book, *Who am I?*, Bhagavan Sri Ramana Maharshi states, "Desirelessness (detachment, vairagya) is wisdom. The two are not different; they are the same. Desirelessness is refraining from driving the mind toward any object. Wisdom means the appearance of no object. In other words, not seeking what is other than the Self is detachment or desirelessness; not leaving the Self is wisdom." In a 1955 edition of the text, the passage appears thus, "Not to desire anything extraneous to oneself constitutes vairagya (dispassion, detachment) or desirelessness (nirasa). Not to give up one's hold on the Self constitutes Jnana (Knowledge). But really, vairagya and Jnana are one and the same. Just as a pearl diver, tying stones to his waist, dives down into the depths and gets the pearl from the sea-bed, even so every aspirant, pledged to vairagya, can dive deep into himself and realize the precious Atman (the Self)."

The passage above stands self-evident in its clear meaning and advice for those who are in earnest about Self-Realization. The reference to "no object" relates to the Knowledge of "no creation," the Realization that the Self alone is and that there has never been anything else. When one abandons the objective outlook, illusion ceases and the Self is known. The rest of the passage explicitly exhorts the aspirant to experience the fusion of detachment and Knowledge by relinquishing the pursuit of what is extraneous in the vain hope of achieving happiness or peace in such a manner and, instead, turning within to abide in their real source by knowing the Self. In practice, this means becoming detached and finding that the poise in the Self and detachment toward all else are of the same degree and are of the same nature. Nothing is alluring. In practice, one turns or drives the mind inward to find the source of happiness in the Self. As the inquiry deepens, one perceives that he, himself, had been driving the mind toward illusion, for illusion has no power or reality of its own, and, if one ceases to do so, Knowledge dawns. Indeed, the freedom of complete detachment is of the very nature of Liberation.

The Six Essentials

The next requisite for Realization is actually a combination of a number of factors that are instrumental in spiritual progress with Self-inquiry. This combination is known as the six essentials. The six are all interrelated among themselves and are interwoven with discrimination and detachment in the practice of Self-inquiry.

Peacefulness

The first essential is known as peacefulness. It is tranquillity and composure. Sankara defines it as "resting the mind permanently on one's spiritual objective and detaching it from all that is sensed."

Peace is of the very nature of the immutable Self, yet, when in the throes of misidentification, one does not seem to experience it, just as though the sun does not really vanish when there are dense clouds, one who is in or under the clouds does not see it. When one places undue importance on the things of the world, when one is attached to one's own ideas, and when one conjures up one's own emotions, one disturbs one's own innate peace. When one depends on the changeful, peace is lost sight of, as peace can be only in that which at no time changes. With such dependence, peace is not or is very insecure, and external changes are delusively viewed as either desirable in the hope of different phenomena causing a better state of mind or as threatening in the fear of the transience of all things. Change is of no consequence to the Changeless. The Changeless alone is one's true nature.

Following the whims of the mind, its desires and fears, offers no peace. Applying the mind steadily toward the purpose of Self-Realization leads to peace, and the very practice of such yields considerable peace in one's experience. If one is composed in oneself, the vicissitudes of the phenomenal life do not overwhelm one. Such composure belongs to those who are focused upon the goal of realizing the Self, the means being of the same nature as the end, which is the innate peace of the Self. The composure is being equanimous in the midst of all things and is directly related to detachment.

One should abide in equanimity in the midst of all occurrences. If there is loss of peace, it is due to attachment and lack of discrimination. These should be thoroughly practiced and meditated upon in order for there to be equanimity. One should not ignorantly disturb or preclude peace by fostering and adhering to one's opinions about things, events, and other people. By the practice of equanimity, abundant opportunities to inquire are found. One's mind is introspective and does not engage in futile interactions that only lead to creating burdensome karma. By peacefulness, one's interactions become beneficial, and the world, with its events, ceases to be conceived as an obstruction to one's spiritual advancement.

Self-inquiry yields supreme peace, yet peacefulness, itself, is integral to the successful pursuit of the inquiry. To set aside the frantic antics of the ego-ridden mind, if only for the reason of desiring to dive within to realize, is peacefulness. To abstain from concocting the brew of ignorance, craving, and frustration or anger or hatred is peacefulness. To be peaceful within oneself and to relate to others on the basis of peacefulness and not unnecessarily agitating the mind enables one to better pursue the inquiry to know the Self.

Meditation on what has just been stated will endow the aspirant with the quality of peacefulness, both within and in relating to others. One should meditate upon being the unmoving, ever-peaceful Witness of all, the Self, of the nature of Consciousness, and so attain peace.

Self-control

Self-control is the second of the six essentials forming the third requisite. Sankara declares its significance to be the control of the means of sensory perception and the means of action.

By self-control is meant the ability to direct one's mind, speech (interactions and communications involving words) and bodily actions wisely. When a person is in ignorance and is overwhelmed by his own delusion, even self-control is lacking for him. The actions thus taken are thoughtless, foolish, impulsive, compulsive, and productive of bad karma; the ways of relating are also karma-producing and, being tainted with attachment, manifest as increasing bondage; the ways of thinking are erroneous and unreasonable and lead to further and further delusion. Lacking self-control, one generates and spins in craving, frustration or anger, and blind ignorance.

Without self-control, even if one knows better, he does not do so. Being introduced to deep teachings, he does not retain them. Knowing of love and compassion, he or she seems unable to consistently relate on that basis. Though life is short and the opportunity to engage in that which is spiritually beneficial is rare and precious, through lack of self-control one squanders one's effort, energy, and time upon worthless things. Without self-control, one's life and experience seem driven as it were by forces beyond one's control, like dried, dead leaves before strong gusts of wind. Without self-control, one becomes arrogant and egotistical, thus missing the opportunity to develop that extremely beneficial quality of humility. Without self-control, it appears that those things that are actually inert instruments and vacuous illusions, such as the mind, the senses, the body, and the world, are one's masters. The seeker of Self-Realization, therefore, seeks to govern himself.

For the aspirant on the path of Nondual Knowledge, self-control is a conscious directing of oneself. It is not the conjuring up of imaginary battles with one's body, senses and mind. It is, rather, contemplating how to best use these instruments to support one's spiritual practice and deliberately acting upon that contemplation while deliberately ceasing to follow the previous habitual patterns of conduct. Self-control will manifest for the seeker as a positive sense of self-discipline and a directing of oneself to all that is spiritually uplifting. It is based upon the recognition that ignorance is ultimately a matter of choice and is self-produced, as are all its manifestations. Because the responsibility is entirely one's own, freedom is also entirely one's own. If it were not so, that is, if one were not entirely responsible for one's own illusions, one could not be entirely free; in other words, Liberation would not be possible. But if one exercises the power of directing oneself in a wiser and wiser manner, Liberation is not only possible, but, with Self-inquiry, it is revealed to be the natural state of the Self.

If the seeker does not exercise this self-control, either there will be no solidity of the endeavor to have the manifest life shine with the light of Knowledge found in meditation or there will be no meditation at all. The first will mean one's life is governed by whims and random opinions. One will experience the extremes of good insight contrasted with states of delusion in which it is as if the insight had never occurred. The second option means no interruption in the samsara, the repetitive, illusory cycle of birth, suffering, and death. While Self-Knowledge, being unborn, One without a second and devoid of causality, cannot be said to depend upon a meditation practice, for the Self and its Knowledge of itself depend on nothing else whatsoever, still, where can someone be found who has Self-Realization, not merely a conceptual grasp of intellectual theory or a mere memorization of spiritual terms, who has not engaged in intense meditation? Such meditation is Self-inquiry, which should be carried on in an intense, consistent manner by those who desire Self-Realization.

Renunciation

The third of the six essentials is known as renunciation. Though this may or may not be carried out in a formal way with spiritual symbolism or vows, the spirit, or true practice, of renunciation is an essential support of the inquiry to know the Self.

This renunciation on the path of Nondual Knowledge is also known as the cessation of action and the withdrawal of the senses from the external. Sankara has defined it as the nondependence of the mind on anything external.

For those who practice this nondual Self-inquiry, there is no set of specific actions essential for this spiritual path. No particular action can be proclaimed to be universally applicable to all seekers, let alone at all times, yet the aspirant's actions must be guided by the spirit of renunciation. Moreover, Liberation from the imagined bondage is a matter of Knowledge and is not a matter of performing certain actions. No action can produce Realization. Knowledge alone yields Realization, and, indeed, Knowledge is itself Realization. It is a path of Knowledge that yields the state of Supreme Knowledge. This understanding is the cessation of action, that is, the cessation of dualistic action-orientation in one's practice. The mere reduction of bodily activities is not what is meant and such would be unrelated to Self-inquiry and Self-Realization. Nevertheless, one might very well renounce worldly activities, useless activities, and unnecessary activities to provide more time for meditation and the receiving of spiritual instruction, and this would yield tremendous spiritual benefits.

The cessation of action, as above described, in this renunciation naturally leads to the Knowledge that one is not the body. Disidentification from the body implies the corollary understanding that one is not the performer of action. The body alone is active, and the Self is free of movement, change, or action. This is renunciation of doership.

Renunciation is part of every aspirant's practice. Detachment must become total for complete spiritual freedom. Renunciation is its expression or reflection. How that expression manifests varies among those who are detached, but there is always some expressed renunciation. It is not reasonable to say that as one liberates oneself from attachment and ignorance that one will still maintain every action and habit, cling to every object and relationship, and continue to harbor the same delusive notion of possession as previous to such spiritual development. When a person joyfully and wisely relinquishes old habits, objects, and such for the purpose of spiritual advancement, such is known as renunciation.

Renunciation is born of contemplation upon the source of peace and happiness. It is born of observation of the facts of life and death. It is born of recognition of the futility of worldly gain, be it objects, wealth, fame, or anything similar. It is born of meditation upon the dreamlike nature of the experience of the world. It is born of meditation upon the transitory nature of all things. It is born of the intense yearning to know and be the Truth at any cost. It is born of the comprehension that clinging is worrisome bondage and detachment is blissful freedom. It is born of the Knowledge of the immediacy of the Truth of the Self.

Nondependence of the mind on anything external means to no longer have one's state of mind determined by outer circumstances, such as how many or few one's possessions, whether or not one's desires are fulfilled, or whether or not situations are to one's liking. Even more so, it is the abandonment of seeking happiness externally based upon the clear discernment (discrimination) of the real source of happiness. It is the means for the equanimity called peacefulness. Further, it means the cessation of the projection of the sense of happiness, reality, and identity upon things extraneous to the Self, which is the abode of happiness, one's true identity, and the one Reality. It is the abandonment of superimposition of the attributes of unreal things upon the Self. When the mind turns inward in search of true Knowledge, regarding outer so-called knowledge as just so much ignorance, the delusive collection of opinions and insubstantial concepts, such is renunciation in Knowledge. Ultimately, this nondependence or renunciation, as it is known in practice, is of the very nature of the space-like, formless Self as realized in Self-Knowledge.

Fortitude

The fourth of the six essentials is fortitude. This has been described also as forbearance, endurance, and the ability to withstand the opposites of phenomena such as pleasure and pain. It is also described as being always free from anxiety or lament over those phenomenal opposites or any afflictions and remaining in a state of equality without struggling for revenge or redress.

Self-Realization itself is effortless, as it is the innate, natural state of the Self. It is Existence pure, and there is no effort required for Existence, nor is there anyone apart from it to apply such effort or to desist from such effort. When ignorance veils that Existence so that there seem to be two states, that of Realization and the unrealized state, and so that one seems to be an individual apart from that Self, an effort is made to end that ignorance. Cessation of ignorance is the purpose of practice on the path of Knowledge. It is the reason to inquire. It is not the attainment of any new thing, but the removal of ignorance by Self-inquiry to reveal the ever-present Reality of the Self to which the effort is applied.

Though there is, in Truth, nothing obstructing one's Realization of the Self, it is usual in the course of spiritual practice to experience obstacles. These obstacles are the tendencies in one's own mind, manifesting as attachments and such. Due to the long-standing habit of misidentification and attachment, such tendencies may not necessarily be destroyed upon the first meditative examination of them. The obstacle to one's freedom seems to remain or to return even if one has glimpsed beyond it. The seeker must, therefore, apply effort with perseverance.

In meditation, the mind may not be steady in its introspection. There may be a plethora of ideas, idle daydreams, or disturbing repetitive concepts. The aspirant must have endurance and apply the necessary strength to overcome these so that the precious opportunity of meditation is not lost upon such meaningless or binding mental delusions.

In phenomenal life, events and circumstances are a mixture of the pleasant and the unpleasant, the pleasurable and the painful, the fortunate and the unfortunate. To realize the immovable Self, the aspirant for Liberation must develop the power of inquiry, the spiritual fortitude, to not be swayed by such transient circumstances. Freedom from being swayed means detachment and equanimity. If, at first, one is caught in the storm of being buffeted by such external phenomena, to persevere in inquiry and meditation until one is no longer so swayed is fortitude. The body is undoubtedly subject to the experiences of pleasure and pain. To inquire so as to no longer suffer thereby, to no longer be so much bemoaning one's plight that one does not take the opportunity to turn within, is spiritual fortitude.

Forbearance signifies freedom from lamenting or making a grievance over what does not please one. One can cultivate a forbearance or non-reactivity toward persons, situations, and experiences that previously upset him, at least to the degree sufficient for the opportunity to commence discrimination regarding the real source of happiness and peace. It is, though, easily and directly attained through clear discernment as to the real source of happiness and peace. In either case, the aspirant develops forbearance, and this results in an absence of suffering due to things and events in the world. It results in not bemoaning what has happened in the past, including absence of seeking any sort of revenge against those who have done something not to your liking, and not being anxious over what may or may not occur in the future. All such delusions are based on the false belief that the world is real and the misidentification with the ego, the desires of one's own mind, and the body. A seeker of Realization cuts these delusions down with Self-inquiry while bringing forth from within the fortitude to address all of this delusion, adamantly refusing to blindly follow the tendencies that would drive the mind toward such grief, anxiety, resentment, seeking redress, and such.

The way of samsara is to cast the responsibility and the blame for one's own experience upon the world rather than to recognize that suffering is self-created and oneself alone can destroy it. For Liberation, the aspirant does not want to carry the mode of approach used to create samsara into his attempts to transcend it. If he does, the aspiration is hampered or becomes interminable. If the mode of mind is dissolved and replaced with the fortitude here described, the obstacles are destroyed by practice of the inquiry, and Self-Knowledge is realized.

The strength in spiritual practice ultimately derives from the immutability and indestructibility of the Absolute Self, and the forbearance from the transcendent, unaffected nature of the Self. Strength of practice comes by practice itself. Strength leads to greater strength; perseverance to a great ability to persevere.

When confronting an apparent obstruction in one's spiritual practice, be it an external circumstance or an interior mode of mind or concept, one is set with a choice. The aspirant can either carry forward with fortitude, by applying himself more intensely than previously to the spiritual practice and perhaps redirecting the efforts in a wiser way than previously through clearer inquiry, or he can abandon the practice. In the latter case, there may be a temporary, emotional relaxation as the seeker begins to settle and stagnate in the familiar quagmire of worldly ignorance. If this state of affairs is further exacerbated by the tendency to misapply nondualistic terminology to it, the seeker will actually take pride in falling into ignorance and will begin to concoct all sorts of absurd interpretations of the essential teachings and invent all sorts of explanations to account for the mentalities, emotions, interactions, and such that are not found in the true freedom of Realization. It is a state of indolence mistaken for peace. Provided the seeker does not exacerbate the situation by claims to a superior state in such a way, he will, sooner or later, tire of the recurring ignorance and will again commence spiritual effort, with greater fortitude than before, for no one can be fully satisfied except in the natural state of complete Self-Realization. If the situation has been exacerbated as above mentioned, the egoism of such will first need to collapse before genuine spiritual progress resumes. The direct path is not to take such a detour to begin with and, with unremitting enthusiasm and energy, pursue the Knowledge of the Self, led on by increasing joy and freedom, until the Self is conclusively realized.

For those who, with fortitude and endurance, turn within to realize the Self by Self-inquiry, that which is indomitable and indestructible is revealed within them.

Faith

The fifth essential is known as faith. It is also defined as a clear understanding and as an affirmative attitude of mind inclusive of humility, sincerity, earnestness, single-mindedness, reverence, and an unwavering determination to find the Truth at any cost.

Sankara defines this as "ascertainment of the scripture and instruction of the Guru with conviction about their Truth, that by which Knowledge of Reality is obtained."

Faith is considered to be the belief in something that is yet unseen. In the path of Knowledge, the aspirant is concerned with the transformation of faith into conviction, and that into the certitude of Self-Knowledge by virtue of Self-inquiry. It is the development of a clear understanding and a conviction in that which is understood. Such may be said to be faith fused with wisdom.

The Truth does not accept the arrogant into itself, for it is egoless by nature. So, only those who are endowed with humility and who hold it in highest reverence realize it. Those who hold the teachings in deep reverence retain them. Those who are humble find their egos to be insubstantial and their own true nature to be formless and vast like space.

Sincerity and earnestness are necessities in the pursuit of Supreme Truth. With insincerity, who fools whom? If one is in earnest to find the Truth, he will be always undaunted and will destroy the illusory fetters that appear to keep him bound, so that his deepest yearning is fulfilled.

Being single-minded in the pursuit of Self-Knowledge comes to those aspirants who recognize the utmost importance of realizing the Self, understanding that in no other way will one abide in enduring peace, genuine freedom, and unending joy. The conviction in the Truth drives one to realize it. If one's own mind is undivided concerning this, that is, if faith is beyond doubt regarding the fact that the Absolute Self, indeed, exists and is realizable, the inquiry into the Self rests upon solid ground.

Faith can be in the existence of the Absolute. Faith can be in the Knowledge of Truth that reveals that the Absolute and one's own Self are identical. Faith in the nondual teachings that reveal this identity is of immense help. Once one has a conviction in them, one can directly experience that Truth for oneself by inquiry into the nature of the Self, and this inwardly verifies the Truth in which one originally had faith. Faith can be in those wise ones who have gone before and realized this Knowledge and in those sages who, having realized, proclaim the Truth and the way to realize it within oneself. Faith in one's own ability to realize, when fused with the humility mentioned earlier, is in keeping with the Truth that all are only the Self and there is no one who cannot realize it. If one has a Guru, the faith mentioned by Sankara is of the nature of the deepest trust. The result of faith in the Guru's instruction, which implies full practice of it, is the Realization of the Self in which one's own identity, the Truth, and the very Being of the Guru are one and the same.

In a path of Knowledge, faith is generated from hearing the teachings and meeting with those who practice them or who have realized their meaning. Faith is generated when reading the instruction left behind from earlier times. Though a certain degree of faith may be needed to even start a spiritual practice—one cannot be so enamored of one's own doubts that one cannot even make a try at it—the practice, itself, will yield the conviction in Truth and in the means to be adopted for realizing it. From a higher perspective, faith is an intuition of one's True Self or natural state, and its strength is derived from the irrefutability of Reality.

In Self-inquiry, faith merges with deeper understanding. In nonduality, faith is further strengthened by discrimination. When faith is joined by the practice of inquiry, it becomes conviction. When conviction is joined with direct experience, it is Knowledge.

Deep, Profound Meditation

The final of the six essentials is profound meditation. What is implied is an inwardly concentrated meditation. What is explicit is that it is a formless meditation. It is sometimes referred to as a practice of samadhi, a state of intense absorption in the Absolute.

Sankara has defined this as the perfect establishment of the mind (buddhi) always in pure, nirguna (attributeless) Brahman (the vast Absolute).

Meditation is invaluable for discovering and securing for oneself experiences of deeper spiritual states and for inquiry for Self-Knowledge.

In a path of Knowledge, meditation consists of Knowledge and the primary means of experiencing such Knowledge is Self-inquiry. Knowledge is formless. It is ignorance when one mistakes sensations, moods, emotions, thoughts, and any other mental phenomena for Knowledge. When one believes that such are knowledge, one is prejudiced by the unexamined beliefs in the reality or truthfulness of the senses (the process of sensation) and of the objects of those senses; one also believes something is so because one has thought of it. Inquiry reveals the invalidity of such—their utter nondependability for discerning reality. Indeed, for purposes of fine discrimination, that which is conceivable or an "object of thought," has the characteristic of unreality. Therefore, for real Knowledge, one must know That which is not an object of the senses or thought, and the means of knowing must not be a mere sensation or thought construct. So, the meditation must necessarily be of this same nature of formless Knowledge if it is to be fruitful. If your meditation itself assumes the existence of the ignorant limitations that your are attempting to transcend, how can it be of much help? If your meditation is that of Self-inquiry, it is not concerned with the products of the senses or of thought, and it is not relying on such for Knowledge. Only an inquiry to know oneself can be regarded as truly inward, and, as such, it is preeminently useful for Self-Realization. Self-inquiry is the significance of this deep, profound meditation.

Concentration per se is not deep meditation. Deep meditation, though, implies being concentrated. If one's attention is usurped by every wayward thought, is compelled to run with every idea and whim, and is caught up in every daydream the mind can imagine, when will there be the opportunity to meditate in order to gain Knowledge of the Self? When one is aware of the purpose of life and aware of the purpose of meditation, concentration manifests. It is just as, when one's life is in jeopardy, one does not at that moment become lost in idle daydreams or meaningless mental imagery. Similarly, when the aspirant is aware of the importance of Realization and the importance of meditation, aware of how to fulfill life's purpose within the ever-narrowing window of time left for it and aware of how precious is the opportunity to meditate on Truth and set oneself free, concentration is present in the meditation. Tracing and holding the sense of "I" as taught in Self-inquiry will simultaneously produce one-pointed concentration and deep, profound meditation. The concentration is, ultimately, actually derived from the undivided intensity of Reality itself and the Self's innate transcendence of all thought.

Samadhi is always a state of absorption, a merging or dissolution of one's identity. In some descriptions, samadhi is classified in various ways, yet, in samadhi itself, no such classifications or the means to conceive of such exist. If the state is prompted by or is inclusive of some differentiation, such as meditation on the whole universe being pervaded by That or the Self as the universal Witness, it is savikalpa, that is, "with differentiation." If it is prompted by meditation of the nature of nondifferentiation, such as the Self and the Absolute are identical or the Self alone is and there has never come to be any objective thing whatsoever, and is an undifferentiated state, it is known as nirvikalpa, "without differentiation." Such is characterized by an absence of illusory, objective perception, inclusive of time, space, and matter. It is bodiless and without mental activity. If the absorption is so complete as to eliminate the possibility of an alternative, a samadhi of Knowledge of the Reality in which there is no such thing as an existent unreality, the natural state of the Self as it innately is without any further effort to be applied or anyone to apply it, it is, as the Maharshi stated, Sahaja Samadhi, which is the natural, innate, effortless state. This is Self-Realization. It could be said that savikalpa retains a unity of knower and known, the meditator at one with the ideal or object of meditation; nirvikalpa is a dissolution of the knower and the known; sahaja is "no creation" in which there are no such things as knower, knowing and known. The experience of all these is available for those who one-pointedly focus on the inquiry to know the Self, though the sahaja state is alone the final goal, a goal which is found to be at no distance but to be one's very Being by those who realize the Self.

Though the Absolute Self is not dependent upon any condition or state of mind, being ever transcendent of all modes of mind and the mind itself, and though Self-Knowledge is thought-transcendent, or free from thought, it is extremely rare to find anyone who has realized this who has not engaged in deep, profound meditation. Meditation should be understood as the invaluable opportunity to be awake to Reality, the chance to be with full focus on the Truth of the Self, the auspicious moment to dismantle and destroy the illusions of the ego, and the time to turn the mind from its own delusive creations to the clarity of understanding what is true. It is the opportunity to be with oneself, not in relation, response, or reaction to anything else, but to see clearly what one's Self actually is, free of every supposition. In the profound Knowledge that thus shines, one finds that there is truly no alternative state, and the meditation is found to be perpetual. Meditation, as Self-inquiry, should be practiced by the aspirant for Liberation until there is no possibility of ever being bound again and the Truth of the Self has been conclusively realized.

There are innumerable forms of meditation. Meditation that does not have Self-Knowledge as a clear orientation will not result in Self-Knowledge. If one meditates upon worldly interactions, one may improve those transient interactions, in a changeful universe that is akin to last night's dream, to a certain extent. If one meditates upon sensations, gross or subtle, one will come to dwell temporarily in those transient sensations. If one meditates upon thought or in a thought-dependent manner, one will arrive at a corresponding mental state, which certainly cannot be eternal. If one meditates by Self-inquiry, the result is Self-Knowledge, or Self-Realization. That is the nondual Self, upon realizing which there remains nothing more to realize, the freedom of which leaves no trace of a possibility of bondage, the perfect fullness of which leaves no dissatisfaction whatsoever, the timelessness of which cannot be measured or terminated, the formlessness of which has no comparison or contrast, and the Reality, or Existence, of which leaves no other existence.

The prime way of developing meditation ability, assuming one has access to nondual teachings, is to meditate. Even if there is no such access, if one ardently meditates with sincerity and the intense desire to realize, the inquiry will make itself known within, and if, one perseveres in the inquiry, the Self, which is one's true nature, will be realized.

The Desire for Liberation

The fourth requisite for Realization is known as the intense desire for Liberation. Sankara has said, "It is the desire to free the mind from the bonds extending from the ego to the body created by ajnana (ignorance) by means of Knowledge of one's own real nature (svasvarupa), not indulgence of the mind."

The desire for Liberation functions as the fuel for one's spiritual practice. If all sorts of spiritual attributes are present, even the other requisites above mentioned, but there is a lack of desire for Liberation, actual advancement, as determined by the degree of freedom from misidentification, will be slow, if at all. If, though, the aspirant would have none of the other requisites or beneficial attributes, but was endowed with an intense desire for Liberation, the other needed requisites and such would manifest in due course of the practice of Self-inquiry. When the requisites are practiced fueled by the desire for Liberation, the highest good results.

Erroneous interpretations of nonduality may lead one to assert that the desire for Liberation will foster or produce a continuance of duality, for it may posit the notion of something for which to search and the seeking for it. This, though, represents an error in reasoning due to lack of direct experience, for there is no "rule" that Liberation must be conceived or treated as if an objective goal apart from oneself. Since Knowledge of the Self is alone Liberation, ignorance is entirely self-imagined, the Self is forever non-objective, and Knowledge is One with Being, therefore, the desire for Liberation is actually a profound recognition of what truly is one's natural state and the discernment of what is not that natural state. Understanding this results in fervently seeking within. Within is the Self. The desire for Liberation leads one to inquire and to thus know the Self as it is, in which there is no duality whatsoever. For one who is to realize the Self, this inner, intense desire to realize and its corresponding search via Self-inquiry represent no duality or difficulty, but rather attention is focused upon the nature of the seeker himself. When the nature of the seeker is known, revealing an utter absence of the individual and only the real Being of the Self existing, the desire for Liberation has been fulfilled and vanishes of its own.

The desire for Liberation should be as intense as possible. If there is clear discrimination, all the force of the desire for happiness that drives the person's life while caught up in illusion becomes the intense desire for Liberation, as that Realization alone is full satisfaction, the fulfillment and the end of the desire. The more intense the desire for Liberation the more ardently one will pursue the inquiry and the more adamant one will be about retaining the freedom found through detachment and disidentification.

The desire for Liberation means the desire for complete spiritual freedom. It is the indomitable intention to snap the fetters of ignorance that seem to bind one's identity, and consequently one's experience, to what is not the Self, that is, from the very notion of an ego, or the assumption of individuality, to the misidentification with the form of the body. The misidentification is composed only of ignorance. Knowledge of the Self, which is one's own self, and this is Knowledge of oneself being the Self alone and not any of those other things, is the destruction of ignorance and the attainment of Liberation.

That which seems to extend between the Self and the body, deludedly regarded as an ego and illusorily manifesting as the mind, gives rise to bondage. One should free oneself of that bondage, or misidentification, too. The mind itself alone has the ignorance, as the real Self never has any trace of ignorance or bondage whatsoever, and the body has no ignorance, as well. The mind alone has it, so it is said that the mind should get rid of it or that one should get rid of the mind. The desire for Liberation arises in the mind as the intuition of what the natural state of the Self is. This desire causes the mind to examine itself, to relinquish its own imaginings, to destroy its own form, and to find its source or real nature.

"Indulgence of the mind," mentioned by Sankara above, is the pursuit and maintenance of the mental tendencies that are the substance of delusion. Desire for Liberation is contrary to them. To concoct any excuse, ranging from the idea that it is too difficult to the concept that there is nothing that can be done to realize, that perpetuates or validates delusion or bondage is indulgence of the mind. To have unbreakable reasons to be free is desire for Liberation. Lack of self-examination is indulgence of the mind. Similarly, pursuit of worldly desires and diffusion during meditation is indulgence of the mind. Freedom from forcing the mind along the paths of such ignorance is brought about by desire for Liberation. The mind's stagnation in misidentification with the body is "indulgence." Freedom from such comes to those who desire Liberation. Following the whims of the ego, fabricating and clinging to the ego's opinions, and worldly attachment are indulgence of the mind. The desire for Liberation opens a different path, the way to the blissful freedom of Self-Knowledge.

The rise of the desire for Liberation within one is the beginning of the end of the ego and its delusions. It is the motivation for sincere spiritual practice. It is the call of the Self to itself to be awake to itself. The surging higher of the desire for Liberation makes the further development of the other requisites possible. It causes one to develop one's practice and brings one into deeper spiritual experience. The peak of the desire for Liberation is to want nothing else and to place none of one's effort into the creation of ignorance. With inquiry, it causes the veil of illusion to vanish like a mirage vanishing into nothingness.

The desire for Liberation arises within all who consider the facts of life and death, who see the futility of worldly life, who observe the sufferings created by ignorance, who comprehend that they can truly be free, who understand that there is a state of complete freedom and peace in which delusion and suffering are no more, and who are convinced that they can find this for themselves. The rise of the desire for Liberation depends on the settled conclusion that the external world, inclusive of other people, objects (or lack of the same), wealth, fame (personal acceptance or popularity), reputation, situations, and other phenomenal conditions are in no way the cause of suffering or happiness.

The desire for Liberation has never been an obstacle for anyone, though lack of desire for Liberation has caused the stagnation of many. The desire for Liberation prompts the inquiry to know the Self and causes one to discern what Liberation actually is.

Ignorance alone is the cause of bondage, and bondage alone is suffering. If there is suffering, there will be the concomitant desire to be happy, to eliminate that suffering, because misery is contrary to our nature. If there is the clear perception of the cause of suffering being one's delusive bondage, there will be the desire for Liberation. If there is the understanding that bondage is only misidentification or ignorance, there will be the desire for Self-Realization, or Self-Knowledge. The Maharshi has said, "Inquiring into the nature of one's self that is in bondage and realizing one's true nature is Release (Liberation)."

So long as one is bound, there will be the desire for Liberation on the part of the spiritual seeker (or the pursuit of delusive, worldly desires by those who do not know any better). When, through the inquiry, "Who is bound?" one realizes the egoless real nature of the Self which is ever free, the desire for Liberation is fulfilled and ended. The Self was truly never bound and has no separate state of Liberation.

Then, the Truth is self-evident as the only One without a second, without an alternative. Thus, the Maharshi's statement, "Who is to realize what when all that exists is only the Self?" This Truth is realized by those who desire to realize it with all their heart and not otherwise.

The desire for Liberation is ultimately the inner yearning to Be as one truly is. Since Being is neither an object nor an activity, the practice can only be that of Knowledge. The result of the inquiry is Knowledge identical with Being. The desire for Liberation is the motivation for the inquiry into the Self.

Self-Inquiry and Conclusion

The preceding discussion of the four requisites for Realization is pertinent to those who are practicing Self-inquiry. The practice of Self-inquiry will be aided by the development of these, and the inquiry itself causes these to develop in the aspirant.

The inquiry uses discrimination and causes discrimination. The inquiry is strengthened by detachment and brings about detachment from all that is unreal or not the Self. Peacefulness and equanimity give the opportunity to inquire, and the inquiry results in enduring peace and seeing all equally. Self-control allows one to direct oneself toward the inquiry, and the inquiry yields the ability to guide oneself wisely. Renunciation turns the mind inward to inquire while dissolving the bondage to samsara, and inquiry causes one to relinquish the possession of the unreal and the misidentification with the not-Self in light of the nondependent nature of the Self. Fortitude enables one to consistently persevere in the inquiry while overcoming all apparent obstacles, and the inquiry yields the transcendent strength of the knowledge that all obstacles are unreal. Faith in the Absolute enables one to inquire with the support of true teachings and one's own inner capacity, and the inquiry results in the certitude of the Truth of the Self. Deep, profound meditation yields the experience of inquiry, and inquiry, making the meditation profound, reveals that the formless nature of the Self is ever present and not subject to any change or condition.

The requisites may be regarded as several or may be regarded as one whole. They will be naturally present in one immersed in the Knowledge of the Self. It may be necessary for any particular aspirant to meditate on and develop one of them, several of them, or all of them, or they may be found to be spontaneously manifesting in the aspirant as a result of the practice of Self-inquiry. It is for the seeker to examine himself and observe which need growth or deepening. They are all within the context of Knowledge and the path of Knowledge to realize the Self. Basic meditations to foster these requisites are briefly stated here in the description of each requisite. Actual practice will, itself, reveal the actual experience with precision. The best way to develop practice is to practice. The best way to strengthen these requisites is to practice them. The best way to deepen the inquiry is to actually inquire.

This booklet is not intended as a manual for Self-inquiry or as an exposition about Nondual Truth. Therefore, only a brief mention of the inquiry and the Truth are made here in order to place the requisites in proper perspective.

Self-inquiry reveals the nature of one's Existence. Existence is undeniable at any time. Even the attempt to doubt it presupposes its existence. What is that Existence? It cannot be known objectively, that is, as an object of perception or conception. Inquire as to "Who am I?" Negate from your sense of identity all that is objective: the body, the senses, the life energy (prana), the mind (inclusive of all its permutations such as cognitions, thoughts, emotions, memories, abstract ideas, and such), and the assumption of existing as an individual being (ego or "I" notion). That which alone remains and which can never be negated is the self-existent Self, the formless true Being, unborn and imperishable.

Self-inquiry reveals the nature of Consciousness, itself. Consciousness is always present as the silent, immutable Witness and is Knowledge, itself. Inquire by negating the perceiving and conceiving, which are but misinterpretations of Knowledge imagined within the context of dualism (such as subject and object). By this inquiry, come to abide in certain Knowledge, which is the Knowledge of Reality, in which there is neither knower nor known and in which Knowledge is not a function. By inquiry, trace out that which is actually aware. It is not the senses and not thoughts, and it does not dwell in any state of mind. By Knowledge, remove the objectified misidentification regarding Consciousness. That which remains is the nondual, infinite Consciousness, formless and eternal.

With each thought that arises, one may inquire, "For whom is this?" The inquirer should already know that all experience is occurring only within his own mind. The answer to the question will invariably be, "To me." This signifies the return of all sense of reality and identity simultaneously to within, to the "I." Then, one should inquire, "Who am I?" Tracing the true significance of "I," the assumption of individuality vanishes, being unreal, and the real Self alone remains, uncreated, imperishable, and One without anything else whatsoever.

Requisites signify what is necessary. Realization signifies Knowledge of What Is. One thing is necessary: to realize the Self. One thing is real: the Self, itself.

May the aspirants who are instructed in the teachings about the requisites for Realization practice Self-inquiry within themselves and, being liberated from all of the imagined bondage, abide in Self-Knowledge, in unwavering freedom, bliss, and peace, in That as That itself.

Om Tat Sat

References to and other explanations of the Requisites for Self-Realization can be found in the:

Song of Ribhu, English translation of the Tamil version of *Ribhu Gita,* published by SAT.
Vivekacudamani, by Adi Sankara.
Sarva-Vedanta-Siddhanta-Sarasangraha, by Adi Sankara (English translation entitled, Quintessence of Vedanta).
Aparoksanubhuti, by Adi Sankara.
All of the above titles can be obtained by contacting SAT.

Invitation

If you wish to further pursue these teachings of nondual Self-Knowledge and the practice Self-inquiry, you are warmly encouraged to contact SAT (Society of Abidance in Truth).

SAT
1834 Ocean Street
Santa Cruz, CA. 95060 USA
Tel.: 831-425-7287
email: sat@satramana.org
www.SATRamana.org

Copyright 2003 SAT

www.ingramcontent.com/pod-product-compliance
Lightning Source LLC
Chambersburg PA
CBHW072116290426
44110CB00014B/1934